The Art
of Playing
Second Fiddle

The Art of Playing Second Fiddle

Encouraging Teens Who Never Place First

by Ted Schroeder

Publishing House
St. Louis

Library of Congress Cataloging in Publication Data

Schroeder, Theodore W., 1939-
    The art of playing second fiddle.

        1. Youth—Religious life.   2. Self-respect—Relilgious aspects—Christianity—Juvenile literature.   I. Title.
BV4531.2.S37   1985   248.8'3   84-15621
ISBN 0-570-03950-9 (pbk.)

1 2 3 4 5 6 7 8 9 10   MAL   94 93 92 91 90 89 88 87 86 85

To Kristen, Ted, and Naomi,
my favorite teens,
whose honesty gave vision
and whose sensitivity
gave heart to these
words.

Contents

Preface

This collection of first personal "let me tell you how it was for me" vignettes is directed to the teen who is in the game of "be the best" and is not winning, who tries and does not get all A's, who competes and does not get all the trophies. It is for the teen who lives through the frustration of being forced to play second fiddle to the more talented and more able.

I remember considerable pain from my teen years. Certainly the pain was not physical (except for that time I broke my arm), but it was very real, and the memory of it lingers.

Interestingly, most of the pain was self-inflicted. It was produced by a frightening game I got caught up in. I think most teens get caught in the game because of the competition of grades, scholarships, and athletic events. It is the game of being the best. The teen years produce great pressure to be the best—and a few are. Some teens indeed are the best students or athletes or whatever. But a great many are not. Like me, they are good at some things and not at others, sometimes able but often inept, slightly talented but not really remarkably blessed. Failure to be the best produces frustration, and the frustration produces **11** pain—a pain heightened every time another teen is recognized for his or her excellence.

I certainly have no pretension that I can offer simple solutions to the hurts and conflicts of the teen years. But part of the pain I remember was the loneliness of it all. I had no idea others felt as I did. I did not know that others were also struggling to be the best and failing. It would have helped, I think, to have known.

This book will have been successful when a teen can say, "Yes, that is what it feels like"; when he or she can say, "It must be all right to feel that way if this other person did"; and when he or she feels encouraged to share his or her own hurts and frustrations with others.

Certainly our Lord did not lay great expectations on us before He would love us and make us His own. Yet we do exactly that to those we love. Those expectations of excellence, whether external or internal, are the source of much pain during the teen years.

Our teens need to know that God loves them in Jesus Christ when they get the D's, when they come in second or third, even when they feel they have completely failed. This book has but one message: God loves you, child of His. On good days and bad, in up times and down, He loves you with an eternal love, a love that will not let you go.

1. Chuck:
White Shoes

Some people grow big all together. Every part of them keeps up with the rest, and they get everything grown to the right size at the right time. Some people don't grow up much at all, but that is another problem.

I grew up all right. I mean I got bigger every year and all. I even got bigger than most other people, and some people think that is pretty great. But I just couldn't seem to get the act together.

My feet grew first.

When I started high school, I was pretty tall, but my feet were—let's put it this way—my feet were big enough to bring out the comic in people. Like when I went to buy ice skates. The guy in the sport shop there measured my foot. But he didn't even go into the back room like they do when they want you to think they are looking for the right size that they really have to order anyway. He just goes, "Well, I never saw a size 14 skate before, but I could sell you two size sevens." And he laughs real loud. See what I mean?

And then there was the time I was working on a street crew **15** in the summer. We'd sweep up the gravel that another crew had spread on the street the week before. This big guy—he was the boss, I guess. He always sat in the truck and listened to the radio while we worked. He says to me in front of the whole gang of guys, "You know, you'd be pretty tall if they hadn'ta bent off a yard for feet." See what I mean?

Anyway, the high school band got new uniforms. The parents' group that bought them thought they looked pretty snappy. They had maroon trousers and these double-breasted coats. They looked like theater usher outfits to me—but no one asked me.

These girls in the band got the idea that it would be neat if everyone got white bucks to wear with the uniforms. White buckskin shoes were big then. I don't remember why. It was just "in" to wear white bucks and white socks.

My folks went a little nuts trying to find white bucks in my size. "You're not gonna like them," my mom kept saying. But what was I supposed to do? Do you know what I would have looked like with the only pair of black shoes in this sea of white bucks?

We ordered them from some company that specialized in big stuff for big people. "You're not gonna like them," my mom said.

"I'll like them, Mom. I'll like them," I kept saying.

Anyway, they came in the mail—in a very big box. And when I opened the box, I hated them. They looked like two great white whales with laces.

I put them on. I felt like I was wearing the Colorado snow mass. Worse, they were so stiff that every time I took a step they kind of went "Whap! Whap!" on the ground.

"I can't wear these," I said.

"I thought you were gonna like them," my mom said.

But nobody really said what I looked like with them on. I had to wear them in the parade. What else could I do?

After the parade, everybody cheered and said how nice we all did and all of that. My mom sent a picture of me in my nifty uniform to my aunt in Chicago. I guess she thought my aunt would like to see a new maroon uniform. I don't know.

My aunt wrote back. She said how the weather was and all of that. And then she said how nice she thought I looked in my new uniform. She liked the gold braiding, she said.

"But why is my nephew the only one wearing clown shoes?" she asked.

See what I mean?

HOW ABOUT YOU?

Ever feel like the only one wearing clown shoes?

Sometimes something makes us obviously different from others—something we can't hide. We might have a nose that is too big, or hair that just isn't the right color, or a different face shape, or be smaller or bigger than the rest. But whenever anyone pays attention to what makes us different, we feel like we are wearing clown shoes.

What do you do when you feel like the only one wearing clown shoes?

HERES WHAT I DID

At first I was gonna quit the band. I mean, maybe no one would notice if I just didn't show. And then I thought about dropping the uniform in the river and claiming it got stolen so I wouldn't have to march in any more marches. But I supposed they'd find me another uniform.

But after I moped around the house for about a week, my dad suggested that I go talk to Mr. Jackson. He was one of the coaches at school, a big man and a friend of mine. So I thought I'd try it.

First Mr. Jackson told me he knew how I felt since he was big and had had some of the same experiences when he was growing up. That helped a little, but not much.

Then he told me that as far as he was concerned it didn't matter to him if I had big feet—and he was sure it didn't matter to my folks, my real friends, or to God either, for that matter.

I told him that I appreciated it. But I was still the one who had to wear the clown shoes.

But then he told me something that really helped. "Every **17** one has to wear clown shoes," he said. "Look for the clown shoes the other person is trying to hide."

I didn't hardly believe him at first. I mean, some people have everything so together. They are so all right—how could they be hiding something?

"Try it," he said.

So I did.

There was this senior jock I knew. He was captain of the whole world, I think. He played sports and talked to the girls in the hall and drove around in a red convertible. He looked like he just got off a poster that told how healthy it was to drink 14 glasses of milk every day. You know what I mean.

Everything fit together on his body. His nose was the right size, and his feet matched—all of that. Anyway, I decided to kind of keep an eye on him—to watch and see if I could find his clown shoes. I really didn't believe he had any.

After gym class the next day he came over to me. "Listen, kid," he said, "if you don't stop staring at my mole, I'm gonna punch your lights out."

"Mole?" I go.

"Yeah. My mole. You just keep your eyes to yourself."

"I will," I said.

I tried to get in one last look. And sure enough, there near his lip was this black mole about the size of a pencil eraser. For him, I guess, the thing was as big as a pair of clown shoes. I mean, really, compared to my feet, the mole was just a molehill. But for him it was a big deal.

Anyway, I started to make a game of it. Instead of worrying about my feet, I started to try to find out what other people's clown shoes were. Sometimes I could get it right away. People with big noses thought everyone was looking right at their nose. They put their hands on their faces a lot. Guys who thought they were too short hung around with short people and bought shoes with big heels. And girls who thought they weren't big enough on top wore loose tops or vests. Stuff like that.

I found out that you could usually get people to let you know what their clown shoes were. If you just stared at them for a little while, they would almost automatically try to cover up what they were ashamed of. They would cover their faces or their eyes or their elbows or whatever. It was kinda fun.

But out of all of it I learned some important stuff:

1. I learned better that God loved me, in spite of what I looked like. My foot size didn't really matter to Him at all. In fact, He kind of liked me the way I was.

2. I knew my family and my real friends liked me, no matter what I looked like. They liked me for me. They didn't really care how big my feet were or whether I was short or tall or whatever.

3. I learned to pay attention to those things I liked about myself, instead of what I didn't like. I liked being tall. So I got some boots that made me even taller. And I smiled when people said, "Boy, is he tall."

4. I tried to remember that most people paid as little attention to the size of my feet as I did to their moles, their noses, their height, or whatever.

5. I tried to find a good compliment to give to people around me. If I liked the way someone was dressed, I said so. If I liked what they were doing, I told them. It made it easier for them to get along with whatever clown shoes they were wearing. And sometimes they would return the compliment.

6. It still hurt when people wanted to be comics and make fun of my big feet. But you have to understand people like that. Some find their own clown shoes so painful that the only way they can live with them is to make someone else feel bad about theirs.

SOMETHING TO DO

Here are a couple ideas for things you can do when a problem like clown shoes bothers you:

—Sometimes when I am really feeling grotesque, I read what the angel said to Gideon when Gideon was chosen **19** to do a special job for God. "I am the least of the least," said Gideon (Judges 6). God still wanted him, and God did great things through Gideon.

—You might think about who you can talk to about your clown shoes—or whatever causes you to feel like everyone is looking at you, pointing and laughing.

—Find someone who has to wear a really gross pair of clown shoes. Someone who is so different that people make fun of him or her. What can you do to let that person know he or she is loved by you and by God?

2. Vanessa: The Group

Almost everybody at school is in some kind of a group. I mean, not just burnouts and preppies and stuff like that. Besides those, there are lots of little gangs that you either belong to or you don't—depending. Most of the groups are pretty easy to figure out. They hang around together in the halls and at lunch. In fact, they're always together. You almost never see one member of a group without another.

It's pretty hard to get into a group if you're not. I mean, the people in the group know who belongs, and the people outside of the group know they don't belong, but no one has it written down anywhere. You just know. And you never really ask to be in a group. You just kinda hang around with some of the kids from the group, and they let you know if you are in or out. See?

For a long time I was out. I didn't start my school as a freshman. We moved here later. And all the groups were together already. And there I was—this loner in a gathering of groups.

Well, I wasn't completely alone. There are these others who don't belong to any group. They are the weirdos, rejects, burnouts, dorks, and like that, who can't really get into a group. Being **21** among them makes you feel about as accepted as a kid with dirty hands at my grandma's dinner table.

The hard part is knowing when you are "ready" to get into a group. I made friends with this one girl, Dawn. She was in a group of sort of preppie kids, I guess. I thought they might be ready for me, so I hung around with Dawn and some of her group. It was funny. I was there, and Dawn talked to me, but for the rest I might just as well have been a painting on the wall. No one said a word to me. Not "How are you?" or "Drop dead." Nothing.

Don't get the idea that I stayed among the rejects and nerds. No. I made it with a group, all right. But after I did, I kinda wished I hadn't.

One day when I was sitting by myself trying to look like I didn't care if I belonged to a group, this girl named Lisa came up to me and started to talk. I had only seen her a few times before that, but all of a sudden she wanted me to "meet some of the kids." There I was—in the group—and I didn't even know what I had done to get there.

The group was going to meet at the shopping center on Friday night. "You'll have a great time," Lisa said. "We always have a ball."

I was not willing to risk getting bounced out of the group the very week I got in, so I decided I had better show up at the shopping center.

There were about six of us that started to cruise the crowded mall that Friday. I didn't even have a clue about what I was getting into.

At first everything was fine. We walked and talked and eyed the guys who were cruising to look us over.

Then Lisa says to me, "C'mon." I followed her into this store—some kind of gift store or something. Anyway it was all full of pins and buttons and stationery and stuffed animals and like that.

We looked around while we kinda made our way to the back of the store.

"Stand right there," Lisa said in a whisper.

22   "Why?" I whispered back.

"Just stand there," she said.

So I stood. Pretty soon she was moving back up the aisle and I followed her again.

"Wha'ja get?" Carrie—she was kinda the leader—asked as we found the group again.

Lisa reached in her jacket pocket and pulled out a little ceramic statue.

"Not bad," said Carrie.

"Where'd you get that?" I go with my mouth half open.

"In that store," says Lisa, real cute-like.

I couldn't believe it. "You mean you stole it?" I guess I said it too loud because the others started to shush me, and a couple of them giggled.

"Course, silly," goes Lisa. "Didn't you get anything?"

"Me? But I don't steal things."

Carrie laughed. "Sure, sweety. And cows don't give milk. Right? Everyone steals. It's just for kicks. No one even misses the stuff we take."

"But it's wrong!" I protested.

Everyone laughed at me.

"C'mon, let's go," said Carrie, and everyone followed. I was still "but . . . butting" when Lisa grabbed my arm and pulled me along. What could I do? I went.

We ran around the side of this theater near the shopping center. There was an exit door there. Carrie tapped on the door with her finger. Suddenly the door opened. One of the ushers, I guess a friend of Carrie's, let us all in.

"Shhhh," said Lisa.

Her advice wasn't necessary.

The next thing I knew I was sitting in a balcony seat watching this big hairy guy stab a naked woman. Then another guy shows up on the screen and starts hacking people up with a chain saw, believe it or not. I was so grossed out I couldn't even open my eyes.

"Is this movie rated PG?" I asked Lisa.

"Are you kidding?" she goes.

At the beginning of the evening I was just a normal kid. Now I had helped with a robbery, snuck into a theater without **23** paying, and was watching a movie I was not even supposed to see.

Some group I got myself into. I was trying to figure out what I was gonna tell my mom when I called from the police station.

HOW ABOUT YOU?

Ever get into something that turned out to be entirely different than you expected? Ever follow the crowd and find yourself doing or saying something you would otherwise never do or say?

It's pretty hard to be the only one who is even willing to stand up and say, "This is wrong," when everyone else is going along. Sometimes it seems easier to go along than to risk being laughed at.

HERE'S WHAT I DID

I knew that if I got up and walked out of the show, that was it for me and the group. But even if that was not so bad, I knew what Carrie and Lisa and their friends would say about me at school. I'd be called little Miss Goody-Goody and never get in a group again. I would become a reject for sure. And could I stand that?

It had been pretty lonely for me before I got in this group. The burnouts and the nerds were very boring people to be around.

Good old light-fingered Lisa on my left seemed to be having a wonderful time. I could see she was because I was trying to find things to look at besides the screen.

On the other side of me was this girl named Joan. I had seen her around school, but I didn't really know her. When I looked over at her, I saw she had her hands over her eyes.

"Pretty gross," I said loud enough for Lisa to hear.

"It's awful," Joan whispered back.

"Let's go," I said.

Joan nodded, and we got up.

"Where' ya goin'," Lisa goes, pulling at my arm.

24 "Out!" I said.

Needless to say, Joan and I are no longer in the group. In fact, Carrie and her bunch never miss a chance to let us know what they think of us.

But who needs them? We got our own two-person group. And it's OK. We talk in the halls and eat lunch together. Maybe a group with two people in it doesn't amount to much according to Carrie and Lisa and their friends. But it is just right for Joan and me. Maybe we are rejects, but we like ourselves and each other, and we decided that's a lot more important than belonging to anybody's group.

The one thing you can say for our group—we gotta get bigger; we sure can't get any smaller.

SOMETHING TO DO

Jesus warned that sometimes people would hate us and persecute us because we belong to Him. When I was little, I didn't really understand what that meant. And I guess being rejected by a bunch of rejects is not exactly persecution. But it still helps me to read the prayer Jesus said for us in John 17. You might want to read His words when you find yourself alone for doing the right thing.

You might want to read about and pray for those in the world who are really suffering persecution because of their faith.

3. Dan: My Brother

My older brother Jim may be one of the great brains of the century. Just to give you an idea, he sits around with some of his friends and talks about chemistry, believe it or not. He and a couple of his buddies will lounge around in the family room, and one of them will say, "But the exponential formula for that substance is completely different." And Jim will say back, "But the principle is the same regardless of the structure," and all like that.

I think somebody is gonna put out a new book called *Who's Who in America's High Schools After Your Older Brother Jim.*

At least that is what it seems like when my folks and relatives get through talking about him. "He's runner up in the state math competition," my mom will say to the butcher, to the kid in the produce department, to the mailman, and to any stray dog who happens by. And he is. Jim is one super math whiz.

And my folks are always talking about the scholarships that Jim is considering. "Well," says Mom, real casual, "they really want him at M.I.T., but Jim is such a homebody. We just don't know if he'll fit in at one of those Ivy League schools."

See, my problem is not so much with Jim. He's not ignorant about his brains. He hardly ever puts me down. He even helps me with my homework once in a while. And he'll kid me and punch me around a little. And he'll walk with me in the halls at school, even when his own friends are standing there talking. He'll just turn away from them and come over and walk down the hall with me. "How's it goin', kid?" he'll say. "OK, Jimmy," I'll say.

For a brain, Jim's an OK guy. Even my friends like him. I guess I wish I could be more like him.

See, my problem is I'm just not a brain like Jim. I'm not stupid, I don't think. I mean, I get my homework done most of the time. I understand what the teachers say, at least in most of my classes. And I even get some A's and B's sometimes. But I can't talk chemistry or do math in my head. And I don't think any Ivy League—or "Poison Ivy League"—school is gonna be trying to get me to go there.

I guess I don't even want to go to college. I guess if I could do anything I wanted, I'd learn to work on Indy style race cars and be on a crew somewhere. I figure that would be great. To be at the races, move from here to there, make a big car run the best it can—that's what I'd like to do.

But my folks think I ought to be like Jimmy. I mean they don't just say it like that: "Be smart like Jim." But they say things like, "This is our younger son—not like Jim, but still trying," or "We hope he gets his grades up a little. It would sure help us if the boys could go to the same college," or "Things just don't come as easy for him as they do for Jim."

The other day I brought home my report card with a D on it in algebra. It felt like that card weighed about 400 pounds in my pocket. I don't know how I got the D. I thought I understood what we were doing. But when the test came, I don't know, something went wrong. I couldn't get the numbers to come out. And there was this huge D on the report card—standing for Dumb! Dumb! Dumbo!

The worst thing was, my folks didn't even yell. They just sat there with sad faces and hemmed and hawed around for a while. "I guess this will cause us to rethink our plans about your future," goes my dad. He's always saying stuff like that. And my mom: "Perhaps a little less time on the television and a little more in the books might prevent this kind of a thing in the future." My dad: "You know you are not too old to learn from the example of your older brother."

The problem was, when Jim took algebra, he was teaching the teacher stuff the teacher never heard of before.

I ended up yelling at my folks. I don't do that very much. But I told them that I hated school and that I hated Jim and that I hated myself and that I didn't want to talk about it and a lot of other stuff I wish a hadn't said.

I know my folks love me.

I just wish they would let me be me.

HOW ABOUT YOU?

Ever felt like second best?

It's tough to be not quite good enough, to always be compared to someone else who is far more capable than you. It's tough not to be jealous of that person, even to hate him. It's tough not to get down on yourself and give up.

HERE'S WHAT I DID

At first I guess I was gonna run away. I thought that if I couldn't be good enough, then I'd just be gone. Then maybe my folks would be sorry. Maybe they would finally see that I didn't want to be like Jim. I didn't want—even if I could—to be a brain and sit around and talk chemistry. I wanted to talk about the things I liked and go places and do things I liked and be like me, not like Jim.

I thought I might get to another state and get a job at a garage. And if I worked hard, I could learn a lot about cars. And maybe I could make enough money either to go to trade school and learn mechanics or to last until I could join the service and see if I could get in mechanics training there. I even packed some clothes the night of the big fight and collected up all the grass cutting money and change I had lying around my room. I wasn't sure how far I could get on 14 dollars and some cents, but at least I would be away.

29

I prayed a lot that night. First, I prayed that I wouldn't hate my folks. I almost did. I thought they were so stupid. Why couldn't they see? Why couldn't they like me instead of just loving me? I wanted them to like me. And I prayed that I wouldn't hate Jim. I really loved him and was proud of him. I used to tell some of the guys how Jim asked some visiting college professor about a formula in front of the whole student body, and the professor stood there with his bare face hanging out and had to admit that he didn't have any idea what Jimmy was talking about. I didn't want to hate Jimmy. I wanted to love him. But I wanted him to be proud of me too.

I think God helped me. The next morning I knew what to do. First I talked to Jimmy. I told him that I had something important to say, and I told him exactly how I felt. I even told him about yelling at the folks and feeling like I was getting to hate him and them. He listened pretty good. You know, for a brain, he's pretty smart sometimes.

And then Jimmy and me went together and talked to the folks. He told them how he really liked me—not just because I was his little brother, but because I was interesting to talk to and because I could figure things out and because I could always fix things that he couldn't get his fingers to work with. And he told them about how he was jealous because all the girls thought I was cuter than him. I think he made that part up, but it made tears come to my eyes, and my folks' too.

My folks listened when I talked to them. And they tried to say they were sorry. But I told them I didn't want them to be sorry but that I was sorry I yelled at them and I didn't want to do that any more.

And I told them that I didn't want them to be less proud of Jimmy. "Jim's a great guy, and God has given him a lot," I said. "I just want to be happy for Jimmy and not feel bad because I can't be like him."

Things are better now. I don't want to sound like our talk solved the problem like magic, or anything like that. Mom still brags on Jim to anyone who will listen. The other day she was going on and on about how Jim was doing this and how Jim was going to do that out East when she finally figured out that the lady she was talking to couldn't speak any English.

See what I mean?

But we're doing better. My folks helped me buy an old junker car I could work on. Dad even bought one of those big auto repair manuals. I see him reading it sometimes so that he can come out and point to some stuff on the motor and ask me about it. "The carburetor there may need cleaning," he'll say. "Might be the reason she won't start." "Right, Dad," I'll say. "I'll have to break it down and clean it when I get the manifold back on."

But he's trying.

The other day I got that $50 piece of junk to run for the first time. It made a lot of smoke and clatter, and I think some of the cylinders didn't fire too well. But it ran.

I heard Mom on the phone yesterday. "You know our younger son," she said. "He's a miracle worker. He can make anything run."

Good old Mom.

SOMETHING TO DO

Here are a couple ideas for things you can do when you feel down on yourself because others are less than proud of you.

—When I was feeling bad because I had yelled at my folks, these words kept going through my head: "But God has shown us how much He loves us—it was while we were still sinners that Christ died for us!" I looked it up the next day. The verse is Romans 5:8. Maybe you'd like to read it and some of the verses around it.

—You might think of how you can talk to your parents or those who are putting you down. It won't be easy to do the talking, but it might help a lot. Or you might find someone who can understand how you feel—a counselor or a friend—and talk to him or her.

—Perhaps there is someone else with a similar problem you can listen to and encourage.

4. Linda: He Said "Hi" and I Said "Ummm"

Some girls just seem to know naturally what to talk about. I mean, they open their mouths and all these words just keep coming out. You gotta admit that sometimes the words don't make a lotta sense. Like my friend Jenny—she keeps saying things like, "makes me want to vomit" and "totally awesome" and dumb stuff like that. But she can laugh and talk without even thinking about it.

Now when it comes to talking, I do all right when I'm around other girls. I can talk about what's happening in school or clothes and shopping or what guy is going with what girl, and all of that. But even with a group of girls, I probably don't say very much. I am never sure that what I have to say is going to exactly fit in. And by the time I think about it, someone else is talking.

But with a guy, my mouth is like completely paralyzed. Or else my brain doesn't send any talk signals to my mouth. I mean, when a guy says hi to me in the hall, I usually end up looking away or just saying, "Ummm."

Just a couple of weeks ago, this guy stands by me in the hall.

"Did ya get your homework done for biology?" he asks real nice. See this guy, Don, is no Rick Springfield or anything. Jenny says he's kinda dorky.

Anyway, I knew he wanted to talk so I said, "Yes, I got it done."

"Tough, wasn't it?"

"Not too bad," I said.

And then there was this silence while we stood there and watched people go by in the hall. It seemed like we were standing there for about an hour.

Finally he says, "Gotta get to class. See ya."

"See ya," I said.

I thought of a million things to say after he left. I could have asked him about the last test or where he was gonna go over the weekend or about the football game—or even just said something about the weather. But I just couldn't think. I know I turned red. Then I couldn't concentrate on algebra next hour and probably flunked the quiz.

Well, this guy is apparently not easily discouraged because he asked me to go out. But if I went out I'd have to be alone with him for the whole evening. I knew that I was gonna have to go out on a date with a guy sooner or later. Otherwise people would think I was completely weird or a total reject. So I said yes. And he said he'd pick me up on Friday about 7:00 for a movie.

All week I knew that Friday was gonna come too soon. I knew I'd never be ready. How do you get ready to talk to someone person for four or five hours?

I thought about how long it would take to write a speech that lasted four or five hours. The six-minute speech I did for speech class took me six hours to write and about six hours to practice. At that rate it would take me about three years to get ready for Friday.

A couple of times I thought about calling Don and telling him I was too sick to go—and that was no lie.

I memorized the sports page in the newspaper. But I wasn't very sure what an ERA was, or an RBI or some of that other stuff. But I supposed it might be better to say something dumb about sports than to say nothing at all.

Then I tried to memorize one of my brother's joke books. But I could never remember the punch lines. I could get the story all right—about this guy who went to the doctor or the guy who hit the golf ball in the water. But I couldn't remember how the joke ended. Is a half a joke better than no joke? How was I supposed to know?

Don picked me up at 7:00, just like he said, and we did pretty good with conversation for a while. He asked me questions and I answered them.

"How about the show at the HiPointe?"

"Fine," I said.

"How about that football team?"

"They're very good this year."

"Do you like Mrs. Kramer for algebra?"

"She's all right."

And things like that.

By the time we got to the movie, I knew we were pretty much in trouble. We stood in line and mostly didn't talk. He smiled at me once in a while, and I smiled back. Then we got inside and stood in the lobby with the people waiting. I guess he was out of questions, and I could not think of one RBI or one joke or even a half a joke.

He kinda put his arm around me in the show, but we didn't say much. Once he asked me if I wanted some popcorn. I said no.

On the way back home he asked me if I liked the movie. And I should have said something about how the plot fit together with the characters and how the acting was good in spots but the leads seemed more interested in making an impression than in playing the parts and how the last movie I saw the star in was much better because he seemed more natural and how I thought the money he was making was going to his head and that if he didn't straighten out he was going to lose his fans . . .

"It was fine," I said.

He took me to the door.

"Thanks," I said.

35

"That's OK," he said. "You sure don't talk much for a girl."
See what I mean?

HOW ABOUT YOU?

Ever been tongue-tied?

It's awful to know you are supposed to say something and to have nothing to say. And the harder you try to find something to say, the dumber the things you think of to say sound. And pretty soon the silence gets so long that anything you might say is gonna sound like it came straight from the turkey's mouth. What can you do when you find yourself tongue-tied again?

HERE'S WHAT I DID

At first I decided that I would never go out on a date again. I would become like a nun or hermit. I would lock myself in my room every weekend and not eat or drink but only meditate. But I knew that was not gonna bring me anything but trouble with my folks.

Then I thought I would watch some of the other girls more closely and see how they did it. Then all I would have to do was to imitate them, and I would be all right. Well, it was easy enough to see what Jenny and the others were doing. They were just saying whatever came into their heads. They were just making words and laughing a lot.

I tried it with my little brother. I made him pretend he was taking me on a date. We sat in the living room, and I just talked while he listened for a while. Finally he wanted the quarter I had promised him. On the way out he said, "You know that stuff you were saying, Sis? It was really dumb."

Now I'm no genius, but I figured the best thing to do with a problem like mine was to find someone with one like it and to find out how she handled it.

So I looked around for an adult who is pretty shy. And I discovered that one was the counselor at high school, Mrs. Braxton. She gets up and talks in front of groups, and all of that. But she always blushes, and I noticed that she kinda hurries along and doesn't hang around and talk with the other teachers much.

I was right. She told me about how she had been shy in school and had the same trouble talking to guys. The first thing she told me was that I was not going to be able to turn into a person like Jenny, no matter how hard I tried. I was what I was, and it was best to make the best of that. She told me that God made some people who could talk really easily, and others were more quiet; they just didn't say much. But I knew that already. I wanted to know what to do about it.

And then what she said helped me quite a bit. She said that I needed to stop trying to think of what to say and to start thinking about what the other person was saying. If I was with another shy person, that person was probably trying to think of what to say as hard as I was. So what I would want to do was help that person find something to say.

That meant:

1. I had to listen to what the person did say. I needed to remember that what the person was telling me was important for him to talk about. Like when Don asked me about my biology homework—he probably didn't want to know about mine, but he probably had something to say about his. All I had to do was give him a chance to tell me about it.

2. I would need to try to find out what kind of person I was with. After a date or an evening with another person, even though I didn't really do it, I should be able to write a couple of paragraphs about that person. I should know what he likes and doesn't like, how he spends his spare time, what kind of music he likes, what good and bad things have happened to him lately, what exciting things he is planning for the future—and stuff like that. And you can find out all of that by asking questions and listening to what he says as he answers. Then all you have to do is say when you feel the same or different.

I can't say that what Mrs. Braxton shared with me changed my life, exactly. I mean I still feel all tongue-tied around some boys, especially guys I really like. I still suffer through a lot of silence when I am with someone for a fairly long time.

But last week I had a date. We went to a place to eat and then to a dance. When I got home, I wrote down everything I had found out about him that evening. And it was quite a lot. I **37** found out, too, that most people really like to talk about themselves—sometimes they tell you even more than you want to hear.

But best of all, that whole evening there were only a few times when I sat there and didn't know what to say.

At the door Mike said to me, "You're kinda quiet, but you're nice to talk to."

See what I mean?

SOMETHING TO DO

The other day at Bible class someone read about Moses in Exodus 4:10-11. I had forgotten that he was a stammerer—that he couldn't talk very well. When I got home, I read some more about him in the early chapters in Exodus. I found a lot of encouragement in the remarkable things God did through that person who didn't talk very well. You might too.

For practice listening, you might spend some time talking with with an older person (neighbor, person at a nursing home, shut-in, etc.). Ask questions and see what you can find out about him or her.

See if you can find someone who is shy and has overcome it—or who is shy and could use your encouragement—and talk to him or her.

5. Paul: Playing Fourth Trumpet

I never thought I was Al Hirt or Dizzy Gillespie or anything like that, but I did take trumpet lessons for about 27 years, or something. I used to take the streetcar every week to Mr. Rioco's office, upstairs from the Laundromat. It always smelled like soap and hot clothes there. I'd huff and puff on the horn, and he'd count the music and then the money I paid him. I never knew if I was getting anywhere or not.

When I started high school, I knew I wasn't gonna make the varsity squad in much of anything. I was pretty good at chasing down my brothers, but not much at handling footballs or things like that. Anyway, I decided to try for the band. After all, I'd been practicing so long my dad used to get a headache when I just got out the trumpet. I didn't even have to play a note or anything.

The day before band tryouts, I practiced until my lip felt like chopped liver. Maybe I overpracticed—I don't know. I wanted to do good. It is really embarrassing to get up in front of somebody to play the trumpet and all that comes out is a kind of whooshing sound.

39

Mr. Bonner, the band director, gave me a piece of music to play. It was a march, I think. But I'm not too good at sight-reading music. I do all right if I like know the melody. But playing it cold . . .

I asked Mr. Bonner if he could kinda hum the melody. He looked at me funny. "It's a march," he said. I don't know if that meant it didn't have a melody or that you don't hum marches.

"Just play it," he said.

Well, I did my best. I counted and blew and got most of the notes. What came out didn't sound much like a march to me. I guess it didn't sound much like a march to the director either. He gave me another piece to play. Even though the new piece had a different title, it sounded a whole lot like the first one when I played it. Mr Bonner frowned a little. And then he started to putter around with his music. I thought he might tell me to forget the whole thing. I guess I should have practiced more marches, but how was I to know?

"Son," he goes with a smile, "I think we have just the place for you. For the first time in the history of this high school band, we are going to have a fourth trumpet chair, and you are it." He made it sound like a big deal.

I went home. "Mom, Dad," I go, "I'm gonna be the first fourth trumpet in the history of the band." They made it sound like a big deal too. I think my mom wrote my aunt about it. At least she said she was gonna write.

Anyway, the next day when Mr. Bonner handed out the music, he gave out some first trumpet music to some guys who could triple-tongue and blow high notes and stuff like that. He gave some second trumpet music to some guys who could just sit down and play a march—from memory. And one kid with a bent silver horn got third trumpet music. He passed out all the band music, and we started to practice. I tried to peek over on the third trumpet music, because Mr. Bonner didn't give me anything to play from. I thought he forgot.

Then I did a really dumb thing. At break I held up my hand. "Mr. Bonner," I said, "I don't have any music." And, of course, everyone looked at me. Just then I realized I had probably made **40** a big mistake, but how was I supposed to know?

"What are you playing?" Mr. Bonner asked.

"I think you said fourth trumpet," I answered as softly as I could. And right away the first and second trumpets started to giggle.

"Oh, yes," goes Mr. Bonner, "you."

He rummaged around and found a piece of third trumpet music that was like torn on the corners and dirty. "Here, son," he goes. "Try to listen to the others, and don't play too loud."

The other trumpeters were almost falling off their chairs. "Fourth trumpet!" they'd go, and then they'd laugh some more.

How was I supposed to know?

HOW ABOUT YOU?

Ever felt like the fourth trumpet?

It's pretty bad to try hard and not get anything for your trouble but someone to laugh at you—to try hard and not even do as well as those who don't seem to have to try.

HERE'S WHAT I DID

At first I was gonna quit. I mean, who needs the grief? I was having enough trouble just getting used to high school without being laughed at. But maybe Mr. Bonner wanted me to quit; maybe he just didn't have the nerve to tell me.

I thought of some neat ways to make Mr. Bonner and the others feel bad about making fun of me. I thought I might stand up in practice the next day and throw my trumpet through the window and say something like, "See if you can get someone to play fourth trumpet now." Or I could slam my trumpet on the floor a few times, hand it to Mr. Bonner without a word, and walk dramatically out of the rehearsal room.

But I'd either have to pay for the window or get in trouble for being in the hall without a pass. Anyway, Mr. Bonner and the guys who played trumpet would probably not even care. They'd think I was just showing off.

I knew it wasn't gonna be easy to stay in the band. I knew that every time someone heard me hit a wrong note, every time they didn't have enough music to go around, every time they **41** paid any attention to me at all, they were gonna tease me about being fourth trumpet.

I don't always pray as much as I should, and sometimes reading the Bible seems like what we do in Sunday school. But that night when I prayed (and cried), I guess I thought about God in a different way. I was sure then that He didn't care that I played fourth trumpet—and that they laughed at me. He just cared. And that made me feel better.

The next day, when I told my folks, they were sad with me for a while. But my dad did a great thing. He just came over to me and put his hand on my shoulder and said, "Why don't you be the best fourth trumpet player they ever had?"

I don't want this to sound like some kind of a made up story or a movie or something. I never got to be a first trumpet. I never did get my tongue to triple-tongue, and I always needed to know how the melody went before I could play it very well.

But I really was the best fourth trumpet they ever had. And the next year I was a pretty good second trumpet. I could stay with the rest, play the music, even help some of the freshmen with their counting. I think I must have driven my folks crazy with practicing. I took that silly trumpet home every night, clanging and banging it around on the streetcar. I practiced so much that even Mr. Rioco noticed the improvement.

Once after the band played in a big parade (we marched for about six miles, I think), Mr. Bonner was really pleased with the way we played. "Everyone did really well," said Mr. Bonner. "Everyone." And he looked right at me.

I'm glad I didn't quit.

SOMETHING TO DO

Sometimes when I'm really down on myself, I read John 21:15-17—what Jesus said to Peter after Peter let Jesus down and denied Him (remember Luke 22:54-62?). What do you think Jesus might be saying to you when He talks to Peter?

Can you think of someone you can talk to when you are down on yourself or laughed at? Who could you listen to when they are feeling that way?

42

ROCK
ROCK

6. Sue: Gram

Gram was more of a buddy than a grandmother.

Oh, she was old, all right—75, maybe 80. I don't know.

And we sure didn't see eye to eye on everything. She'd scold me sometimes about the way I wear my hair or my makeup—stuff like that. But she did it with a smile. I knew it didn't really matter.

And we'd even argue every once in a while about movies and music. "What kinda racket is that?" she'd say when I had the radio on. "R rated movies?" she'd go. "When I was younger the movies were all rated P for pleasant."

But one thing was for sure. From when I was a little girl, whenever I'd go to her house, she'd sit in the big rocker in the front room. And she'd take me on her lap. And I'd put my head on her shoulder. She always smelled of ginger and tea, and some kind of cream she used on her face. And she'd rock me a little— I mean even now when I was grown. She'd call me her baby. And sometimes I'd cry.

I knew I was too old to get rocked by my grandmother. No one would believe it, even if I told them. But there on her lap, **43** with the smell of spice and her strong arms around me, there I felt safe—safer than anywhere else in the world.

Sometimes things got bad at home—like when Mom and I were not getting along. I don't know if Mom ever had time to rock me. At least I don't remember she did. And Mom always was trying to straighten me out. I guess she meant well. "Do this!" she'd say. "Do that!" Over and over again. And sometimes I'd yell at my mom. I didn't really mean to. But when she'd ask me the same question for the 49th time, or when she'd "talk to me" again about my weight problem. Sometimes I just couldn't help it.

And then she'd be hurt, and I'd feel guilty and mad at the same time. Then I'd go to Gram's.

Gram never told me what to do. I don't know if she always understood what was wrong. But she'd let me cry. And she would love me. Things were always better when she would hold me.

That day when I came to her house, Uncle Billy told me that Gram was very sick. I tried to touch her hand as they took her to the ambulance, but I don't think she saw me.

We stood near her bed in the hospital for a long time. One time she opened her eyes and looked at me. I think she said "Baby," but I'm not sure.

They called from the hospital about midnight and said she was gone. I didn't want to hear it. I shut my bedroom door when the phone rang. I got dressed and started to leave the house. I wanted to go to Gram's house and sit on her lap and cry.

But she wasn't there any more.

HOW ABOUT YOU?

When have you lost someone you loved? Sometimes it seems like the people we love are always gone when we need them. It is not only death that takes them away. Sometimes it is distance or divorce or illness.

It is hard to describe the pain we feel when someone we depended on, someone we were close to, someone we needed is gone. It is more than sorrow, more than being let down. It is

44

like being torn apart, like being operated on without an anes-
thetic—part of ourself is removed, and nothing can fill the emp-
tiness.

HERE'S WHAT I DID

After the funeral I went with Mom over to Gram's. Mom
said she had to "go through some papers," or whatever.

I sat in Gram's rocker by myself. It felt too big for just me.
I could still smell the ginger and her face cream. But the chair
was so cold and empty. I rocked a little like she used to. And I
cried so Mom wouldn't hear me. I knew Gram wouldn't care if
I cried in her chair.

I guess I was angry at Gram at first. I felt like she ran out
on me. The day she died, Kathy, my "best friend," told me off
in front of the whole school, practically. Who could I tell but
Gram? Who else would even care? How could she leave me
when I needed her so? How could she just go off to heaven and
leave me with no one to hear me or to hold me or to let me
cry?

And then I was angry at God. Why did He take my Gram
when there were so many old people around who were just
living from day to day? No one needed them. No one would
even miss them. Why take my Gram? Why take her before I
was ready? I knew Gram had to die sometime. But why now?
Why me, God? Why pick on me? I have enough trouble. I have
plenty of hurts in my life. Why give me more? And why take
the one person who could help?

And then I felt guilty. Maybe if I had left school right away
and gone to Gram's, I would have been able to get help for her
sooner. How long did she lie on the kitchen floor before Uncle
Billy found her? Maybe I could have caught her so she wouldn't
have hit her head or helped her breathe—something.

I came home from school, and Mom was singing in the
kitchen.

"Mother! How can you be singing? Didn't Gram mean anything to you? How can you sing?" I knew I was yelling, but I
didn't care.

45

Mom was pretty cool. Sometimes she yells back, but not this time.

"Do you think Gram would want me to stop singing?"

"But Mom, don't you care that she died? She was your mother! Don't you even care?"

She took me by the shoulders and sat me down in front of her. I thought she was going to scold.

"Honey, that old lady was the dearest person in the world to me. Oh, I know we argued sometimes. Mothers and daughters always argue. But I knew this. She loved me. On my good days and bad days, when I was right and even when I was wrong, she loved me.

"She helped me grow. She gave me everything I have. She taught me more than how to cook and clean. She taught me how to live and to love.

"And she taught me how to let go.

"You don't know this. You were too young when your grandfather died. But when she stood at his grave, the tears were still on her cheeks and she was smiling. 'Be happy, Harry,' she said. 'I'll be with you soon.'

"I'm sad that she's gone. There will never be anyone like her in my life. But she's where she wanted to be. She's with her Savior and all the loved ones who have gone before. How can I be sad about that?"

"But Mom, I still need her!"

Mom was quiet for a while. Then she reached over and wiped the tears from my face.

"I need her too, honey. I don't know if I can get along without her. Sometimes the best thing she did for me was to just hold me."

46   "I know," I said. "She would hold me too."

Then Mom took me on her lap, and it didn't feel strange at all. It was almost like I belonged there. And I put my head on her shoulder. She smelled of ginger and face cream. We both cried and held each other. I knew Gram wouldn't mind.

SOMETHING TO DO

Sometimes when Gram was sad, she'd read Romans 8 to herself or out loud to me. When I was little, I didn't really understand the words. But I knew they helped Gram. Sometimes I read them now, especially when I think of her. Maybe they would help you too.

Find someone who has lost a loved one. See if you can be a listener for that person. Or just be there and let him or her know that you care.

7. Alex: Weird Harry

I don't know too much about that stuff, but I think Harry is kinda slow. I mean, he's not falling down stupid like some of the burnouts or those macho guys who think it's cool to walk around with their shirts half off like some kind of a flea-infested ape.

Naw, Harry is OK. He's just not very bright. I mean, you can see him in the classroom early before a test studying his notes and writing stuff on papers. And he always goes in to ask the teacher questions. It just doesn't seem to do any good. He always gets D's or maybe C's on tests no matter what he does. He smiles about it, even makes jokes about being a dummy. But I saw him crying once by his locker after a teacher told the whole class that Harry was the only one who got an F.

And there's something else about Harry. He just can't seem to do things right. It's like he tries to figure out what people would want him to do, but then he does it wrong or weird. He says stuff too loud or laughs at the wrong time or says things like "Come on, guys. Let's go!" And everybody kinda rolls their eyes and gets that "Oh, no" look on their faces.

49

Most of the other guys try to stay away from Harry. I mean, they don't tell him outright to get lost—well, a few do. But they'd probably tell their last friend to get lost if they thought it would make them seem like superman to the girls.

Anyway, the guys sort of ignore Harry. He comes around and stands near when they talk, and sometimes he tries to say something, but nobody pays him much attention. And when they go to leave no one says, "Harry, you ride in my car," or "Harry, you can come with me," or anything like that. It's like Harry is a shadow or something.

And I know what's wrong. The guys don't want to be called weird either. They think that if some girls see them hanging around with old Harry, they'll think they are like Harry, kinda dopey and out of it—and the girls won't have anything to do with them.

The other day this bunch of guys was standing around in the halls when Harry came up. One of them says, "Hey, Harry, did ya get your crotch shot yet?"

"Crotch shot?" says Harry real interested.

"Yeah," says the smart kid. "We all got ours last hour. Didn't they call you yet?"

"No," says Harry. He didn't even seem to see that some of the guys were laughing already.

"Well, you better get over to the nurse and tell her you want your crotch shot. They musta forgot you."

"Are you sure I'm supposed to get one?" says Harry as innocent as a baby.

"Oh, yeah," they all told him with only half-hidden grins.

I stopped Harry before he got to the nurse's office. I told him it was all a joke. But Harry didn't laugh. I don't think he even understood what they told him—or why. I didn't laugh either.

So, you know how it is with Harry. I sometimes think how Harry feels about it—I mean with people walking around him and not listening to him and playing what they think are jokes on him.

Funny. Harry doesn't seem to complain much. He still smiles **50** and says hi. He's always friendly to me. And the other day when my locker jammed, he came right over and tried to help me get it open. And then he made room for my books in his locker until I could get mine open again.

I think Harry would like to be my friend. But I don't want everyone to think I'm weird. I think Harry needs a friend. No, I'm sure Harry needs a friend. But does it have to be me?

HOW ABOUT YOU?

Know anybody like Harry?

There are probably lots of Harry-like people in your school—in every school. They are the ones who just don't quite fit in. They aren't so different that people feel sorry for them; they are just different enough that people don't want them around. Maybe they are fat, or slow like Harry. Or maybe they dress funny or they don't know how to act just right.

It must be tough to be like Harry. It must hurt a lot when people turn away. But it's tough to help too. It's hard to like a person like Harry—even harder to do something to help.

HERE'S WHAT I DID

I don't want you to think that this was an easy problem for me. I mean, I have enough trouble getting along with the guys without weird Harry hanging around me all the time. And most of the girls treat us like we got the plague when Harry is riding shotgun in my car.

But I sure don't want to hurt Harry. He gets hurt enough. I know God made us all different, and it would have been easy for me to have turned out like Harry. I guess all of us are about a half a step from being really weird anyway. And if I was Harry, then where would I be?

I tried talking to some of the other guys about Harry. "He's just strange," they said. "Just don't worry about old Harry," this one guy said. "He likes being that way or he'd change."

I guess I don't believe that. I don't think Harry knows how to change even if he wanted to.

The other day in church they were reading that part of the Bible that tells how a bunch of Jesus' followers left Him. I guess they thought He was strange too. I mean, He just wasn't what **51** other people expected Him to be, and they walked out on Him. "Will you go away too?" He asked His disciples.

I couldn't help thinking of old Harry when they were reading about Jesus and His disciples going away.

I wonder, you know, if God had something important to do right today how He might not pick Harry to do it. God didn't always pick the brightest and the best to do His work when He had a job that needed to be done. It sure would be the pits if God picked Harry and I couldn't even be his friend.

I decided that I couldn't just treat Harry as if he wasn't there. God made us both. And just because I think that God made me better doesn't mean I can go on as if Harry was nothing.

I had a talk with Harry. I told him I'd like to be his friend, but I couldn't hang around with him all the time. I had other friends too. And that seemed OK with old Harry.

And I figured that even if I look a little weird for being around Harry, maybe Harry looks a little less weird for being around me and some of the other guys.

So I tell Harry he can come in my car. And I try to remember to call him up once in a while.

But it's not all that easy. Some of the guys bug me about being around Harry too much. "You're gonna turn into a spaz like him," one of them says. And the girls don't talk to me and Harry much when we walk down the hall.

But I know this about Harry. If my car breaks down, if I need a quarter to make a phone call, if I need someone to pick up a book I left or someone to even watch my little brother on a Friday night—Harry will do it. And he'll even have a good time doing it.

Maybe that's another reason God might pick Harry if He had something important He wanted done.

SOMETHING TO DO

Look for the person you know who is most like Harry. See if you can let that person know that he or she is important, that you don't care that he or she is different, that you would be willing to have that person as one of your friends. It won't be easy. But you may get a better friend than the ones you lose for doing it.

HOO BOY

8. Karen: My Plan

I am definitely not in danger of being mistaken for a movie star. It's not that I'm ugly or gross or anything like that. I think I look pretty good when I get my hair curled right and my makeup on straight. But some people don't seem to help me have much confidence in my looks.

I once told my grandma that I thought I wasn't very pretty. I thought she'd give me some encouragement. "You're very pleasant looking," she said.

And my aunt—she's always bragging about her kids to whoever will listen. She looked me and my sister over and said to my mom, "It must be great to have such plain looking children. At least the boys won't be chasing them all the time."

I'm not sure how "pleasant looking" and "plain" stack up against pretty or beautiful, but a knockout I am not.

But my aunt was wrong. Some of the guys at school do pay attention to me. Some of them tease me, and some try to talk to me in the halls or after school. The only trouble is that the ones who are interested in me are the ones I am definitely not interested in.

One is this guy they call Spider. I don't know why—maybe because he's creepy. Well, he's always hanging around pulling my hair or pushing me. He's a real geek, you know. Just to give you an idea—I don't think he's ever shaved. I mean, he doesn't have a beard, just all these long stringy hairs all over his face. He looks like he's moldy or something. The other day he stopped me in the hall. I think he was going to ask me out. But I real quick told him that I had to meet a teacher and got out of there. He's such a jerk. And he's the one who's after me, believe it or not.

Well, there's this other guy, Randy. He's not real cute or anything, but he's "pleasant looking" enough. And he's so nice. He talks real soft and always helps people. He seems like he would care about somebody besides himself, and he wouldn't do a lot of dumb stuff like pulling hair and other completely weird things.

But Randy doesn't know I'm alive. I mean, I meet him in the hall and smile. He says hi and walks right on by. I know he's not going with anyone. I asked around. No one has even dated him.

I tried a couple of simple things first to get to talk to him. I dropped my books right behind him when he was digging in his locker. He turned around and smiled at me. "Hi," he said. Then he picked up my books and handed them to me. "See ya," he said and he was gone.

Obviously something more direct was needed.

I told my friend Kris about the whole thing. She's into some guy named Brian—and she can't even see anyone else. But she said she'd talk to Randy about me. I made her promise not to tell him that I put her up to it. She was just supposed to sort of find out how he felt.

The next day I saw Kris and Randy talking at lunch. They were laughing and just having a great time. All of a sudden I thought I might have made the great screwup of my life. What if Kris dropped Brian and grabbed onto Randy? What then? I'd have to kill myself. What else? I sure wasn't going to go with ape-man Brian.

But it all worked out all right. Kris told me some stuff about

Randy—where he lived and all. And she said she asked him about me real casual, so he wouldn't think I put her up to it.

"What did he say?" I couldn't wait.

"He said he didn't know you very well."

"That's it? That's all he said?"

"That's it," she goes.

Big help.

I was ready for something more drastic. All this dinking around was getting me nowhere. This called for a grand plan. I had to get him into a situation that would force him to talk to me. But how?

First, since Kris had told me where Randy lived, I thought I might drive by his house and kinda accidentally drive up on the front lawn. He'd have to talk to me then. He might even ask me to help him reseed the lawn. But I threw that idea out. His dad might have a heart attack with my car planted in his front yard. And Randy might not be very impressed with a girl who can't keep a car on the street.

The other ideas I had weren't much better. I thought about pretending his car hit me in the parking lot. But with my luck, I'd probably get my foot under the wheel and end up in the hospital.

One night I almost called him and told him I was at home alone and someone was after me. But he might not care, and then where would I be?

My master plan came to me in history class. From my desk I could see Randy walk down the hall every day going from gym class (he was excused for a while because of a pulled tendon or something) to the library. If I timed it right, I could tell the teacher I was sick, get a pass to the nurse's office, meet Randy in the hall, and faint right in front of him. Then he'd have to do something. He might even carry me to the nurse. And, of course, we could talk on the way.

The plan went pretty good at first. I got the pass by saying I felt like I was going to throw up. Most teachers are not crazy about kids throwing up in their class. You can get a pass pretty easy if you just hold your hand over your mouth and look as green as possible.

55

I met Randy coming down the hall, just as planned. As he got near enough to say hi, I did this collapse, neatly on the floor in front of him.

"What's the matter?" Randy said as he started toward me.

Just then I hear "Let me do it!" from the classroom across the hall. And who is coming on the run? None other than our great friend Spider!

"I've got first aid training," he hollers real loud. And sure enough, Randy backs away.

"Get back! Get back!" yells Spider like a paramedic at a 12-car crash. Of course, by now he has gathered quite an audience.

"I'll take care of this," Spider announces even louder, and he pounces on me like a starving cat on a wounded bird.

And you'll never believe this—he starts to give me mouth-to-mouth resuscitation!

I thought I'd die. His mouth was over mine, and he was pinching my nose so hard my eyes started to water. Good old Randy stood there and watched, and half the school applauded when I came to in a big hurry.

While Spider took a few bows, I didn't disappoint my history teacher. There, right in front of everyone, I threw up—right on Randy's shoes.

HOW ABOUT YOU?

Ever want something so badly you were willing to risk anything to get it? Ever plan something and had it completely backfire on you? Ever try to impress someone and end up driving them away?

It's hard when you like someone and they don't even know you're alive. And its even harder to try to let someone know you like them without making a fool of yourself or making them hate you instead.

HERE'S WHAT I DID

I thought I'd die there in the hall. There I was looking at Randy's shoes that I had just thrown up on, with the taste of Spider's tongue still in my mouth.

I thought Randy would never speak to me again. After all, how ignorant can you be? I got up and ran. I didn't even get a pass or stop at my locker. I just ran home.

"What's wrong?" asked my mom as I got to the door.

"I don't feel very well," I go as I head up the stairs to my room.

"What's wrong?"

"Nothing. I threw up at school—that's all."

"I knew it would happen," goes Mom. "Eating all that junk food all the time. What did you have for lunch? Candy bars again, I'll bet. What do you expect from your stomach when you put all that sugary stuff in it all the time?"

"Oh, Mom!" I yelled. "You just don't understand!" And I slammed my bedroom door and turned on the stereo loud enough that she couldn't hear me crying.

First I thought about changing schools. Maybe I could start out again somewhere else and no one would know me or what happened in the hall outside history class. Maybe there would be somebody like Randy at the new school who would just like me.

Dumb old Randy—what was the matter with him? He just stood there and let that jerk jump on top of me. Why didn't he grab Spider by the collar and throw him out the window or something? No. Good old helpful Randy just stands there long enough to get his shoes thrown up on.

And I wished I was dead, or gone, or on some other planet. I wished I could get plastic surgery and join the army. I just wanted to be anywhere but back at that school.

My mom came in and tried to cheer me up. She listened when I told her what happened. Of course, I didn't tell her that I had it all planned to get Randy to notice me.

"Just sleep on it," she said. "It will all look better in the morning."

I didn't even want to think about morning.

Just then the phone rang. Mom got it. It was for me.

"Find out who it is." I didn't want to talk to anyone from school.

"Some guy named Randy," my mom goes.

I started to run to the phone, then stopped. Maybe he was gonna yell at me for ruining his shoes or something.

"What does he want?" I called to Mom.

"He wants to see if you're all right."

We talked for a while. He did ask if I was all right. But I was feeling like such a nerd. How could I have done it? How could I have gotten that desperate?

I couldn't stand it. "I have something to tell you," I said.

There was this long silence at the other end. I knew he was waiting for me to say something. I had to or I couldn't face him again.

"I did it on purpose," I said.

Another long silence. "What? Throw up?"

"No, the faint. I did it on purpose to get you to talk to me."

I thought he'd probably hang up, or laugh at me, or yell. "Well, it worked," he goes. "I guess we're talking."

"But I feel so bad. Will you forgive me?"

He laughed a little. "Sure. There's nothing to forgive. No one got hurt or anything."

"But I made such a fool of myself." I was almost crying again.

Randy thought a little. "I guess you'll have to forgive yourself then," he said.

He met me at school the next morning, and we walked around together. Some of the kids were kinda ignorant about what had happened, but not Randy.

We're good friends now, Randy and me. Not like boy- and girlfriends. Just friends. We talk and study together sometimes. I'm glad I met him.

But I really wouldn't recommend my plan. If you really want to meet some guy, you'd better do something besides throw up on his shoes. Some guys just don't go for that sort of thing.

SOMETHING TO DO

Sometimes our plans do hurt ourselves and others. Things can easily go wrong, and somebody ends up in pain because of what we have done. Then it is important to ask forgiveness from the person we have hurt and from God. Then we need to believe that we are forgiven so that we can forgive ourselves. When I'm feeling that I've done something unforgivable, I like to read 1 John 1:9 and Psalm 86. Maybe they will help you too when you need to be forgiven and to forgive yourself.

Find someone you have hurt, someone who carries a grudge against you, and ask forgiveness. And then find someone it is hard for you to forgive and ask God to help you set aside the hurt that person has caused you and to love him or her again.

9. Mike: Who Is That Guy They See in Me?

This psychologist they sent me to sat there scratching his chin and reading the report from the school counselor.

"Your grades seem quite constant," he said.

I don't know what that meant. Both he and I knew I was in his office because everybody thought my grades ought to be better.

I didn't say anything. He seemed nervous. I thought psychologists were supposed to be able to talk to people. Why should he be nervous?

"To what would you attribute your constant underachievement?" he asked with his eyes on the desk.

Underachievement? Pretty classy word. I had been called many things. Lazy was my dad's favorite word. Mom usually came up with something like dreamy. Now I had graduated to underachiever.

In any case, this guy was waiting for an answer. Should I tell him that I think that most of the stuff I have to study in school is dumb, draggy, and pointless? Why should I care how many **61** sonnets Shakespeare wrote or how many soldiers died at the battle of Gettysburg?

Should I tell him that the teachers are petty and unfair? that some just can't teach their subjects? that the books we use are silly and out of date? that the subjects we study have nothing to do with what's important?

Should I tell him about the terrible tiredness that comes over me every time I have to write a paragraph for English or study some formula for geometry?

Should I tell him about the time I spend with my star charts and computer programs?

Should I tell him how much it hurts to fail—especially to study for a test and still get a bad grade because the stuff just doesn't seem to want to stay in my head?

Should I tell him that sometimes it is easier not to try so that I have an excuse when the bad grade comes?

Should I tell him how much I hate that person in me that my folks want me to be—that stranger with my name who always studies, always does the right thing, always wears his clothes the right way, always keeps his room cleaned up, always gets good grades, always speaks respectfully to his elders, always is eager to do anything that adults suggest?

Who is that guy? I never agreed to try to be that guy. Why does everyone want to make me into something I'm not? Why can't they take me for what I am? Maybe I can't always get the best grades, but do I have to hate myself for that? Maybe my room is a mess, but maybe I like it that way. Maybe my hair is too long—or at least too long for those who think they know how people ought to wear their hair. It's my hair.

Maybe I like being what I am. Maybe underachievers are really people who don't want to play the game adults seem to think is so important—the "be the best" game.

Why do I have to be the best? Who cares who gets the best

grades, the best scholarships, the best college entrance test grades? Who cares who gets the trophies and honors and recognition?

I don't want it! I don't want to be the best anything! I just want to be me and not that goody-goody wimp they are trying to make of me!

I ought to tell this guy. I ought to yell at him and tell him to leave me alone, to paint "underachiever" on a big square sign and stick it up his nose! I ought to bang on his desk and tell him to mind his own business . . .

"I don't know," I said.

"Hmmm. Very interesting," he goes as he scratches his chin some more and looks at his shoes. "We'll have to go into this problem in a little more depth."

I thought I might throw up.

HOW ABOUT YOU?

When do you feel the pressure to be something you are not, to play the "being the best" game, to live up to the expectations of others? How do you feel that pressure? How does it make you feel?

It's pretty tough to be constantly told that you are not quite good enough, to bring home five B's and one C and be told to work on the C, to be told that a little more effort on your part would make you closer to what those others think you ought to be. But you know you will never make it because that other person is perfect, and perfect is impossible for someone who is constantly failing to "live up to his potential," as they say.

HERE'S WHAT I DID

When I left the psychologist's office after about an hour of not answering his questions, I had the urge, like always, to run away.

Whenever I got ready to run away, I always imagined Mom and Dad sitting at the kitchen table with a picture of me in front of them. And Mom would be crying great sad tears. And Dad would be shaking his head and saying, "We should have **63** appreciated him more while we had him. Now he's gone and we'll never be able to show him how much we loved him," or something like that. Pretty dumb, I know. But you can't help what you dream—even daydream.

But that's the trouble with running away. I never really did it because, I guess, somewhere inside me I knew it was a dream. I knew that I would not be able to go out west and find a job as a cowboy or something where I could ride out by myself for days and no one would yell at me or tell me what to do or criticize me. Somehow I knew that place and that job were as unreal as my dream about my folks crying over my picture.

But it was also pretty clear that if running away wasn't going to solve my problem, the chin-scratching psychologist wasn't either.

So I went and talked to Smitty. Smitty is what people call a character. He had been my buddy when I was little. He always had a piece of candy and a smile for me whenever I would go to his "appliance repair shop." You knew it was an appliance repair shop because it was full of appliances. The place was packed with toasters, waffle irons, can openers, clocks, radios, and whatnot, stacked to the ceiling. And everything there had two things in common. All of them didn't work, and all of them were waiting for Smitty to get around to fixing them.

Smitty looked like a beardless Santa Claus with a crew cut. And he was just about as popular with the kids in town. You'd see him sitting in the grass, cross-legged like an Indian, his pudgy hands resting on his pot belly. And there would be a dozen kids around him listening to him tell a story or just laughing.

And it was funny. For all the love he got from children, he got just as much criticism from adults. They'd shake their heads when they saw him talking with the children. "Doesn't he ever get anything done?" they'd say to no one in particular when they saw him on a bench just visiting with whoever was there. "He'll never amount to anything," they'd say as he nodded off again in the lounge chair out behind his shop.

Smitty smiled at me when I told him the psychologist called me an underachiever.

"Want a piece of candy?" he said as he settled himself to listen to me.

"No," I go, "but I need a little advice."

Smitty smiled again. "Advice I got," he said.

He listened to all I had to say.

Then he said, "You know, son, for a long time I was a try-harder person. Every morning I'd look at myself in the mirror and tell myself I had to try harder. I had to try harder to get my work done, to be what people expected me to be, to stop spending so much time talking to children, listening to people, and watching God's good creation become whatever it was He was making of it.

"And every morning I would wake up disappointed with myself that I had not been able to be what I was supposed to be.

"Then one day I was watching some birds build a nest. And the Bible passage 'Freedom is what we have—Christ has set us free' kept going around in my head. The birds were free. They didn't have to try to be anything but what they were. They built their nest exactly as they were supposed to. They never tried to make it bigger or in a different shape. They never tried to build it out of better materials or to make it more impressive to those who watched.

"Right then I finally understood what God's free love in Jesus meant. He did not love what I could make of myself. He loved me—just the way I was. Even if I was as simple and unimpressive as the bird on the branch and what I did was as uncomplicated as a simple stick nest.

"For years I had been trying to build a nest that was not mine. It was the creation of all those try-harders who were telling me I ought to avoid the things I liked the most.

"I surely don't think everyone should be like me. Some people would call me lazy. And for sure I will never amount to anything according to the try-harder folks. But I'm happy with me. I like my life and what I do. And I enjoy looking at myself in the mirror in the morning."

Maybe Smitty was putting me on a little. Maybe he was looking for a good way to explain the fact that a couple hundred **65** appliances were still waiting for him. But he did help me to see that the most important thing is that I be happy with what God made me. As long as I am ashamed of what I am, I will always be hurt by the criticisms and expectations of others.

I talked to my folks the next day. I didn't yell at them or anything. And I didn't try to blame them for my troubles. I just told them what I thought I was and what I could do. I told them I needed their encouragement and support, not criticism. I told them that I might not always be the best, but that was all right with me. And I might not always be what they wanted. I might not be as neat as they wanted, or I might not always get A's instead of C's. But even if I could not be the best, I would be the best me I could.

Don't get the idea that one talk with my folks solved everything. But we do talk now. And that is the best part.

And since I thought about what I could do, I stopped being afraid of what I could not do. And the studying, the tests, and everything got easier. Not that every paper is an A. But I can handle the C's and not be ashamed of them. And that is a good feeling.

Maybe I'll never build a skyscraper or a shopping complex or even a big house on the hill. But maybe, with God's help, I can build a nest that fits me.

SOMETHING TO DO

Sometimes when I don't feel like I'm worth very much, I like to read 1 Corinthians 12 and 13. It tells me that every person, even me, is given gifts. And the gifts that really matter are those I can use not to get good grades or to impress people but to help others. Maybe the encouragement will help you too.

Spend some time finding out what talents and abilities God gave you. Don't look at how they compare to others; just find out what your own gifts and abilities are. How can you use them in the best way?

Talk to your folks (teachers? counselor? pastor?) about how you see yourself and what you would like to accomplish in school and with your life. How does that compare with what they see

for you? Talk about how the two pictures can get closer together.

10. Marie: My Dad

No one expects parents to be perfect, but sometimes, honestly, you'd think they would catch onto some things.

Like my dad. He used to be my buddy. I mean, we could relate and all of that. We never really talked a lot—at least not about stuff that really meant something. It was mostly a lot of blah about the sports and stuff at school and like that. But we had a good time together when we went to the ball game. He'd explain this and that to me about why this guy stood wherever and why that guy went in for another. I'd pretend to know what he was talking about. And he'd say to his friends, "She's really inta baseball, for a girl."

Not that Dad's a real brain or anything. He's just a working guy. He's been at the same factory for I don't know how many years. He doesn't talk about work much. But he's kinda into sports—football and that stuff. And he's a pretty good bowler. He used to take me along to the bowling alley once in a while. I'd sit and watch, and get a little bored. And he'd buy pop and hot dogs for me. I don't think he ever explained much to me about bowling, but I knew I was supposed to clap and smile **67** when he got all the pins down. And I would because I liked my dad, and I wanted him to think I was OK. I wanted him to be proud of me.

I remember once, he went out of town to this bowling tournament. He came back with this big gold trophy he'd won. It seemed like it was about a yard tall when he put it in my hands. "Here, Princess," he said. "This is for you." The trophy is really kinda gross, but it's still on my dresser.

But lately he doesn't seem to know what to say to me. The last time we went to the game it was like almost total silence. He watched and I watched, and he said this and that once in a while. And I'd smile quick and say "Uh-huh," or something. But he didn't feel comfortable, I know. And I didn't know what to do for him. We're so different now. Maybe since I don't go to the bowling alley with him any more, he doesn't really like me. I don't know.

The other night I was really feeling bad about walking by him all the time and never having anything to say. I thought I'd give it another try.

"Daddy, can I talk to you?" I said.

"Not now, Princess," he goes. (He still calls me princess around home.) "I have to walk the dog."

THE DOG! Can you believe it? He had to walk the dog. I thought I'd die right there.

I figured I must be hopeless or something. Maybe dads and daughters just can't talk after a while. Maybe it's just too complicated. Or maybe he's not proud of me anymore. But you'd think I was more important than the dog.

HOW ABOUT YOU?

Ever felt like you're taking second place to the dog, if not with your parents, perhaps with a friend? No matter what you do to prevent it, relationships change. And sometimes it's hard to understand why. Just when you think you are close to someone, they are a million miles away. And just when you think you know where you stand with someone, they change or you change or something changes. And it's hard to know how to fix it, how to make things the way they were before.

HERE'S WHAT I DID

First I thought of 17 different ways to make Daddy mad. If he thought I wasn't as important as the dog, maybe if I did some of the stuff the dog did, I would get more noticed. I couldn't exactly wet the rug. But I could tear something up or get in his way when he was trying to do something else or bother people when they came over to visit or even refuse to eat my food.

I thought about how it might be if I went on a hunger strike. Our dumb dog went on one last summer. The little beast wouldn't eat for about a week. Everyone, including Daddy, was all worried. They bought all different kinds of dog food. Finally they took Poochie to the vet, and he said that the dog would eat again as soon as the weather cooled off—which he did. But what if I really stuck to it. I mean nothing to eat—no nourishment of any kind. I could see myself withering away in my bedroom, getting thinner by the hour. Somehow when I thought about it, I shriveled up into a skeleton in about three days. And everyone, including my dad, would be sitting around trying to get me to eat.

But it never worked out. I tried skipping a couple of meals, but all that happened was that I sat around with a long face and thought about candy bars. Then somebody told me that it took about three months to starve to death. I didn't think I could make it.

Well anyway, I can usually talk to Mom. I mean she is sometimes too quick to tell me what to do, but about some things she can listen pretty good, especially if I tell her that it's important.

When I told her that I didn't think Daddy liked me any more, she said that wasn't true. But she did listen. And she got real quiet as I told her.

"I don't think he meant to say that the dog is more important than you," she said.

"Mom, I know he didn't mean that. But that is what happened."

My mom tried to explain to me about Dad. She said that he grew up with two brothers and that he worked around men all the time in the factory. He really knew a lot about relating to **69** guys, like when he was bowling and all of that. But she thought that maybe he was a little afraid of me, now that I had grown up a little. She thought that he just didn't know what to say to me anymore. He didn't know what interested me, what I would care about, and he probably was afraid he wouldn't be able to answer my questions if I asked them.

I never thought that maybe Daddy was afraid of me. I knew he was kinda shy around new people, and maybe I was a new person to him now that I had changed and gotten more grown up.

Mom said that Daddy wasn't all that good at talking to her either. When they got engaged, all Daddy could say was, "I could meet you at the church some day, if you wanna." I mean, romantic he is not.

The next night I took Poochie for a walk. Then I brought Daddy the leash and asked him to take me for a walk. He smiled a little, like he used to when he told people how good a baseball fan I was.

I won't tell you that our walk was all that great. We talked some blah about baseball and stuff about classes at school and how they were kinda boring.

He told me a little about when he was in school, but we were quiet a lot of the time.

I put my hand on his arm, and he left it there for a while.

When we got back to the house, I gave him a little kiss on the cheek. "Thanks for the talk, Daddy," I said.

Then he smiled and gave me a little hug. "Thanks, Princess," he said.

I think maybe we'll take some more walks together once in a while. And maybe when he goes to the next bowling tournament, he just might bring me another trophy.

SOMETHING TO DO

Sometimes when I am feeling lonely or disappointed in the people I would like to depend on, I remember how Jesus loves me and how He prayed for me. I like to read John 15 then. Maybe Jesus' loving words will help you too.

Is there a way you can help your folks understand you better? Look for a time to talk when they are ready to listen.

Is there a way you can let your folks know you love them and appreciate them? Maybe if you can get the message across, they can do a better job of letting you know how important you are to them.

11. Steve:
The Trouble with Kissing

There's a question that used to just bug me to death, and I could hardly get up the nerve to ask anyone: Just how in the world do you kiss someone?

I mean, I knew about kissing on cheeks and pecks on the forehead. I may even have touched lips with someone sometime, I don't know. But just how do you kiss a girl and mean it?

I felt so stupid to have the question running around in my head all the time. I mean, here are these eighth graders making out in the back seats of cars and all over the place and I was wasting half my life meditating on a simple kiss. I thought I was going crazy or something.

I guess I'm too shy. I mean, I like girls and all. I like to be with them and talk to them. I like them to like me and to be around me. But I still could not figure out how you kissed a girl.

And it's not the kind of question you can ask your mother. I could just see myself strolling into the kitchen and laying the question on my mom. She would have probably given me three vitamins and sent me to bed.

73

And I sure couldn't ask the guys. What would I say? "Say fellas, maybe someone could give me a little lesson in kissing." They would have killed me.

I guess kissing is one of those things you are just supposed to be able to do. But it sure seemed like a big deal to me. I mean, I kept worrying about ending up on a date with a girl who really knew how to kiss. Then how would I have looked? Or would she even be able to tell? How was I supposed to know?

The more I thought about it, the more complicated kissing got for me. There were so many questions:

How do you hold your mouth? I used to practice my pucker in front of the mirror, but it was pretty hard to tell whether I was doing it right.

What do you do with your tongue when you are kissing?

And what if you bump noses? Do you say, "I'm sorry," or just keep on kissing?

How hard do you kiss? Is it better when you kiss harder, or is longer what is important?

See? And how was I supposed to know the answers?

I read this book my folks gave me. It sure told me a lot about how babies happen, but there wasn't much there about kissing.

Judging by the amount of time they spent at it, it didn't seem like the people in the movies had much trouble with kissing. Maybe you aren't supposed to think about things like kissing. Maybe it is something you just do like walking or falling down. After all, what's the big deal? You just put your mouth on someone else's and leave it there for a while, I guess. No big problem—is there? How was I supposed to know?

I asked Mandy for a date. I really liked her. We'd talk and laugh sometimes. She and her friends used to hang around when the guys and I were fooling around in the halls at school. I asked her if she wanted to go to a movie. She said OK.

We had a good time. We saw this dumb movie and laughed a lot. We had a coke and I drove her home. She put her hand on my arm when we said good-night. I think she would have kissed me, I don't know. I wasn't sure—so I just left.

I wanted to ask her out again, but . . . well, sooner or later

I was going to have to face it. But what if I tried to kiss her and missed her? What then? How was I supposed to know?

HOW ABOUT YOU?

Ever worried about a problem that seemed too simple or silly to tell anyone else about? The trouble with those dumb little problems is that they get bigger and bigger the more you think about them. And pretty soon the thing that ought to be easy for you to solve has you completely hung up.

And who can you tell or ask without getting laughed at?

HERE'S WHAT I DID

First I asked my older sister about kissing. Mostly she's a pain, but she dates a lot and ought to know something.

When she got done laughing, she says, "Don't worry about it. It all comes naturally."

Big help there, Sis!

I almost didn't ask Mandy out again. I thought about growing a beard, renting a cabin in the mountains, and becoming a hermit. It wasn't too great an idea though. I hated being alone, and I guess I really wanted to know how to show someone when I cared for her.

We went to the show again. Mandy held my hand, and I put my arm around her for a while. I stalled over my coke because I knew the showdown was coming.

We stopped in her driveway, and she leaned over near me.

I thought about shaking her hand and leaving or looking at my watch and telling her I had to run or turning on the radio or starting a conversation about the last football game or something.

"I want to kiss you," I said. I couldn't believe I was saying it, but Mandy didn't seem to mind. "I want to, but I don't know much about it."

Mandy smiled. "Neither do I. Maybe we could try."

Listen, let me tell you something. Kissing is no big deal. Anyone can do it.

Like they say, it just comes naturally. **75**

SOMETHING TO DO

Some problems seem too silly and unimportant even to bring to God. Somehow it seems that He ought to be interested only in big problems and big mistakes. When I feel that way, I like to read about Jesus' miracles. Just look over Matthew or Luke and see how many times Jesus helps people with what must have seemed to Him like little problems. And He cared about little people too. You can read about that caring in Matthew 19:13-15. Sometimes it helps to remember that while no problem is too big for God, no problem is too small for Him either.

12. Sarah:
Second Place Trophies

Katy and I have been in the same classroom since we moved here when I was in second grade. And we've always been "best friends."

It's hard not to like Katy. She's pretty and bouncy and full of fun. She's one who can make me laugh, even when I'm feeling down.

I guess I love Katy, in a way. She helps me and listens to me and talks to me about what is happening in her life. I was the only one she told about Jim, her boyfriend. No one else at our school even met him.

But in a way I hate Katy—and that is the hard part. In everything I can think of she is always just a little better than me. When we take a test, I get a B and Katy gets an A. Oh, she's not ignorant about it. She doesn't wave her paper around and grin like some weirdos. But she just says to me nice, "That's good too," or something. It kinda hurts.

And when we had to make our first speech, Katy told me how scared she was and how hard it was going to be for her to get up in front of the class. She even cried a little bit on the day **77** it was her turn to speak. But she did terrific. Everyone said her speech was great. And when I made my speech, I got stuck in the middle. No one laughed or anything. Katy said to me, "You did real good too."

We both run track, Katy and me. We are in most of the same events. We don't talk about it, but we try hard to beat each other. She's very good. I used to be able to beat her once in a while, but not any more. She seems to get faster without even trying. She doesn't have to work like I do.

I run a lot in the evenings. I have a course around the neighborhood, and I run it maybe twice. It must be about two miles. It makes my legs hurt, and sometimes I get a headache when it's cold out. I know I have to do it though.

At the track meet, Katy and I both won our heat in the 220. I won pretty easy, but Katy slipped a little at the start and almost lost to a girl who really got a jump on her. I felt like such a rat. I was hoping so hard that the other girl would win. It would have been so great to go up to Katy and say "You did just fine" or "Maybe next time" or something like that. But Katy won. And I cheered as loud as anyone. I even hugged her when she came back from the finish.

She didn't even look like she was trying as we ran alongside each other in the final. I was working as hard as I could, and she even had time to look at me for a second and smile. She beat me by three steps. And I cheered and hugged her again.

She told me I ran a real good race. I know I did. I have a second place trophy to prove it. Sometimes when I look at the trophy on the dresser, I laugh and cry at the same time.

HOW ABOUT YOU?

Ever been jealous of someone you'd really like to love? It's hard when the people we like best are better than we are. We don't know how to take them, what to say. Do they look down on us because we are not as good? Do they feel the same way about us—loving us and hating us at the same time?

Maybe it's easier to have friends that are rejects or burnouts. At least they don't always try to show you that they are better. But then again, they aren't very interesting to be around either.

HERE'S WHAT I DID

I guess I just about decided to stay away from Katy. There at the end of the race, I almost cried in front of her. I came so close to yelling at her and telling her how much I hated her for beating me all the time. Why couldn't she let me win? Why couldn't she just fall down or quit? If she loved me, why didn't she give me a chance? But that was no good. If she let me win, I wouldn't really win.

I thought about training even harder. Maybe if I ran 8 miles a day or 10 miles, I would finally be able to beat Katy at something. I could imagine how it would be to win. I could see it in my mind. We would be coming toward the finish, running right together. And suddenly I would take off with an incredible burst of speed—racing forward with power that Katy could never match. And she would stand there at the finish with her mouth open. "How did you ever do that?" she would say. "I could never run like that."

But it was just a dream. Katy was just good—just naturally good. I couldn't take that away from her. I could probably run 25 miles a day and still come in second to her.

But I wanted so much to stop hating her for what she was able to do. I wanted to be happy for her when she won instead of hating her. I really wanted Katy for my best friend.

Then one time we were sitting together at a meet, waiting for our event.

Katy was quiet for a long time. Then she said, "I have a confession to make. I don't want to feel this way any more, so I have to tell you."

"Tell me what?"

"I am terribly jealous of you," she said.

I didn't think I was hearing right. "Jealous of me? How can you be jealous of me? You always win. You always get first place and the best grades. How can you be jealous?"

Katy hung her head. "Oh, those things don't mean anything. Races only give you trophies, and no one remembers grades. You have two parents who love you. And sometimes I hate you for that."

I had never thought about it. It was true. My mom and dad were usually pretty great. They helped me and listened to me. They never put me down when I lost a race or nagged me about my report card. They always wanted the best for me and let others know how much they cared.

I guess Katy didn't have that. Her folks were divorced. She lived with her father, but they didn't get along very well. She never talked about her mother. I think she saw her sometimes, but she never told me about it.

"Sometimes when I'm at your house and your parents are laughing and talking and everyone seems so happy—I just hate you for it. Why can't I have a home like that? Why do I have to be alone most of the time and afraid? Why do you get every-thing good and I have to live with nothing?"

Then I told Katy about how I felt when she won the races and got the good grades. It felt good to tell her, and she wasn't angry or hurt or anything. She just smiled at me. "I'd trade you all my trophies and A's for your home," she said.

I had listened to Katy tell me about her troubles before. She had often said how she argued with her dad and had to take second place to her stepbrothers. But I never knew before how much hurt she had in her and how much she needed me.

Katy and I are still best friends. Oh, she still gets more A's than I do, and I am making a collection of second place trophies. But now when I hug her at the end of the race, I really mean it.

SOMETHING TO DO

Loving friends is never very simple. Our feelings about them get all mixed up sometimes. When that happens, it helps me to remember a real friend who never changes His love for us. Maybe you'd like to read about that Friend in John 15:13-16.

13. Dave: The Klutz

The other day we were watching some guys play professional basketball. There was this center—he must have been about 10 feet tall. The guys on his team would toss the ball in the air, and he would jump maybe two yards off the floor, catch the ball on the way down, and stuff it in the basket, all in one move. "He moves like a cat," my dad said.

He was right. That center was one of those who seem to have gotten all the grace and speed that some of us don't have. It's like they can run or jump even before they think about it. It must be great to be like that.

Maybe all of us are a little like animals—some like cats with grace and speed, others like bulls with power and strength. Me— I'm more like a duck—a flightless, featherless duck.

You think I exaggerate. No really. I don't quack, but my body shape is definitely ducklike. I am kind of round in the middle and narrow on the top. And for all of the hours I have spent working on my walk in front of the mirror—for the life of me I

81

can't seem to get rid of the waddle. See, that's just it. Some guys can jump four feet off the ground, catch a basketball, stuff it in the basket, and land running. Me—I have to practice walking.

It must be great to move and leap and make baskets even without thinking. With me it's different. Picture a duck doing the high jump. That's me. When I say to my legs, "Jump!" they do not immediately lift me two yards off the floor. They do not carry me to new heights of athletic accomplishment. When I say "Jump!" to my legs, they say, "What?"

I wasn't always aware of my ducklike characteristics. When I was very small I just thought I was a little rounder than the other kids. Of course when they ran I always got there last, but that wasn't so bad. It was when we started to play baseball and basketball at the neighborhood playgrounds that my problem became clear to me.

You know how it is when they choose up teams. Usually the two best players get to pick. And they pick the other good players first. I never chose. I never was picked first or second or even fourth. When I was chosen they said, "If we get him, you gotta give us an extra player."

I won't bore you with my deeds of wonder on the athletic field. But there is the neighborhood story that still goes around about the time I finally got a hit in the ninth inning only to trip over second base, do a perfect swan dive toward center field, and crush the shortstop who was trying to tag me for the third out.

Or the time I was running to third base, looking back to see where the ball was—I lost my way and ran over the umpire. He was taken to the emergency room at the hospital to see if my footprints on his chest had cracked any ribs.

Then there was the time I was playing center field. I lost a fly ball in the sun, and it bounced off the top of my head over the fence for a ground rule double.

And the time I fell on the football and broke it.

And the time I swung the bat so hard at a third strike that it flew out of my hand and made this neat little hole in the windshield of the coach's car.

Anyway, you get the idea. All people are not created equal.

I could practice for the next 40 years—11 hours a day—and I would never be able to catch and stuff a basketball. If they threw the basketball in my direction, I would know exactly what to do. But by the time my hands and feet got organized and ready to do what they were supposed to, the ball would have hit me in the nose and gone over to the other team.

See what I mean?

HOW ABOUT YOU?

Ever felt like a duck at a convention of cats, like a turtle at a gathering of rabbits? It's tough to be the slowest, the clumsiest, the most inept. It's hard to see others do things that are nearly impossible for you, no matter how hard you practice or try.

It's hard to be the one who is chosen last, the one who gets only groans when it's his time to bat, the one who always strikes out and misses the plays in the field almost every time. It's hard to be a duck in a world that only applauds the wonderful exploits of people who can move with the beauty and grace of a cat.

HERE'S WHAT I DID

Our comic books always had Charles Atlas on the back. The story was always the same. This poor little guy got sand kicked in his face by this big bully. And then he sends for Atlas's exercise program, and pretty soon he comes and takes the girl away from the bully.

It doesn't work. I mean, I never got sand kicked in my face, but I did send for the book. I even did some of the exercises for a while. I bought some weights and jogging shoes. Not much happened. Oh, I guess I got a little stronger. I probably felt a little better. And I definitely made a bigger breeze when I struck out.

The easiest thing was just to stay away from sports and games. I mean, who needs to be the joke, the last one chosen, the klutz? I had enough trouble in my life without that. I could get along without ball games if it only meant pain.

I got very ashamed of my body. If only I could be like the others with muscles and moves instead of a paunch and a waddle. Why did God make me like that? I surely wasn't any good for anything built like a butterball turkey. It just wasn't fair.

More and more I stayed to myself. I thought no one liked me. I knew the girls didn't like me. They liked the jocks, the muscle men. They didn't like guys who looked like they were put together by a committee, who couldn't even catch a ball, much less a girl.

My mom used to ask me why I was hanging around the house all the time and not out like the other kids. But how was I supposed to tell her that there was nowhere for me to go. No one wanted a clumsy klutz around. I couldn't do anything the other kids did. I couldn't run or dance. I was no good at games, and most of the time the other kids made fun of me. I'd probably still be in my bedroom feeling sorry for myself if it hadn't been for Mr. Watkins.

I met him the night I went with a friend to a youth meeting at another church. It was no big deal, just something to do. But I couldn't take my eyes off Mr. Watkins, the youth leader. He was a guy you'd never figure for a counselor. I mean he was just plain funny looking. He was short and fat and bald. Not only that—he had the biggest nose I had ever seen on anyone. If I looked like him I would have hid in a small closet and never gotten out. But there he was running around with the kids, playing games and having a great time. He'd bounce from this group to that. And he was always laughing. Everything was a ball for him. And the kids loved him.

But the greatest thing about him was that he knew he was funny looking and he didn't care.

They were playing this game where everyone was supposed to take turns rolling this egg along the gym floor with their nose. Now there was no way I wanted to get into that game. I could imagine what I might look like rolling an egg with my backside up in the air. But there was Mr. Watkins.

"Hey, let me give it a try," he says real loud. "Course with my rolling equipment there is really no contest," he goes as he points to his nose and laughs real loud.

After the meeting I talked to him for a while. He was real patient and listened.

"Listen, son," he said. "When I was about your age, I almost decided to kill myself I was so unhappy about the body God had given me. I couldn't do anything. Worse, some of the other guys used to get their kicks just making fun of me. I was so afraid of them, I would spend most of my time at school hiding from them.

"Most of the time I got out of gym class by pretending to be sick or something so the guys wouldn't ride me. But one time I was supposed to climb this rope up to the ceiling. I knew there was no way I was even going to get off the ground. I don't know what came over me, but all of a sudden I started to do this routine about how I was going to climb the rope with one hand and my nose. And all the guys laughed. But there was a difference. Instead of laughing at me, they were laughing with me.

"It wasn't easy, but I learned to laugh at myself. I know I'm funny looking. I can't help that. I know that people will make fun of me if I give them a chance. I asked God to help me love myself enough to be able to laugh at my big nose and funny shape. And it works.

"Believe me, son. If I was ashamed of my looks, these kids would never accept me. They would just make fun of me and shut me out. But they all feel like I do. They all feel ashamed of the way they look sometimes. And they like the way I'm able to laugh at myself. It puts them at ease and encourages them to laugh at themselves. Try it. Like yourself enough to laugh, and others will laugh with you."

Well, I'm still learning. It isn't easy to laugh at yourself. It seems like it will only make it worse, make others laugh more. But . . .

Last week they had this pickup softball game at our church picnic. I was going to hide when they were choosing teams, but I decided to try. The first time up I hit the ball a little, but I heard someone say, "Oh, no!" when I came up in the fifth with three men on. I wanted to disappear or to try harder to hit the ball or just to quit. But as I was picking up my bat, I said real loud, "Look out now for the home run hitter," or something like that.

Everyone on my team laughed with me as I went to bat. I still struck out, but one of the guys patted me on the back as we went out in the field. "We'll get 'em next inning," he said.

I don't want to sound like I have this thing licked. I still want to hide sometimes. I still want to stay in my room and never hear them make fun of my duck waddle or my funny shape. But it is easier now that I met Mr. Watkins. I know that I don't have to spend the rest of my life being ashamed. Maybe I do look like a duck. But God made me that way. Maybe ducks can't leap like a leopard or run like an antelope. But ducks can make people laugh. And maybe people need a laugh more than they need another slam dunk.

SOMETHING TO DO

In the Bible, that little guy Zacchaeus was kind of funny looking. I mean, he was so short that people made fun of him. And Jesus loved him. Even when he was bad, Jesus loved him. Sometimes I like to read that story. Maybe you would too. It's in Luke 19:1-10.

Practice laughing at yourself. What do other people sometimes tease you about? How can you like yourself well enough to laugh about yourself with them?

Find the greatest klutz you know and let that person know that you care, even if others only make fun.

14. Laura: My Friend

About the first of November my Mom starts getting all excited. Not that November's so great. But November means that Thanksgiving is coming, and Thanksgiving means we are going to visit where mom calls "home."

Every Thanksgiving since before I can remember we always pack ourselves and everything in the house that will fit in the car and head for Grandma's. Believe it or not, we even sing "Over the River and Through the Woods" along the way.

I don't think we ever discussed it. I mean, it's just the thing we do at Thanksgiving. And every Thanksgiving visit is like an instant replay of the last. Aunt Gert always says, "My, you're getting so big. It just doesn't hardly seem possible." And Uncle Charlie says, "You're getting to be quite a young lady." And Grandma says, "Why, I remember when I carried you in my arms and changed your diapers. and then she goes on to tell the same "cute" little story about how I took off all my clothes at one of these family gatherings because I said I got too hot in front of the fireplace—or something weird like that. I try not to listen to it. I mean, how many times can you stand to hear about how you bared your bottom in front of all the relatives?

And if I didn't know better, I would bet my life that Grandma had a huge Thanksgiving dinner frozen somewhere, and all she does every Thanksgiving is break off part of it, warm it up, and serve it. It is always exactly the same. The turkey looks the same. "My, that's some bird!" my dad always says. And the sweet potatoes look the same, and the cranberries, the potatoes, the gravy—everything exactly the same.

And after dinner everyone says, "Oh, why did I eat so much?" And they have the same football game on—everything. And the worst part is, after the dishes are done, we have what Grandma calls "sharing" time. That means that all the cousins have to take turns doing a little performance for everyone. My little cousin Mike, he usually spells some words from school, and everyone applauds like it was some big deal. And some of the other cousins sing. Last year my cousin May—she's a little strange in the head I think—well, she recited this very odd little poem she made up all about woods and being alone. Everyone clapped again, but I don't think anyone understood it.

I made the mistake, some years ago, of playing the piano for sharing time. Now I am always saved for last and made to play the piano. It is so totally embarrassing that I can hardly get my fingers to work. And everyone applauds real nice and says how much I've improved over last year.

And Mom loves every minute of it. She waltzes around arranging this and that, asking about this person and that from when she was a girl. She is never quite as happy as when she is "home." She seems to belong there. And as we are driving back every year after the gathering she says, "Now wasn't it just wonderful to have everyone together again?"

This year Robin, my best friend from school, asked me to go with her family to New York over Thanksgiving. And I really wanted to go. I'd never seen a big city like New York, and Robin is an only child and needed someone to go along with her.

But my problem was how to tell Mom. It was November already, and Mom was flying high "getting things ready for the trip home."

I decided to take the direct approach.

"Mom, Robin invited me to go with her and her family to New York for a few days."

"That's nice, dear," she said as she whizzed into the kitchen. "Now where are those plates mother wanted me to bring the next time we came home?"

I followed. "Then I can go with Robin?"

She was digging in the cupboard. "Well, I don't see why not, honey. We know her family real well, and I'm sure they wouldn't let the two of you get into any trouble. We'll talk to your father about it when he gets home. Now what piece are you going to take along to Grandma's to play for sharing time? I think that last one you have been practicing would be just right. It really shows how much you've improved since last year."

"But, Mom," I go, "you just said I could go with Robin. I won't be going with you to Grandma's. I'll be in New York."

I thought Mom was going to drop over. "Not go to Grandma's? We ALWAYS go to Grandma's. You have to go. They are counting on you being there. You wouldn't want to miss a visit home, would you? We always have such a wonderful time there. You couldn't miss that."

"Mom, YOU always have such a wonderful time at YOUR home. This is my home, Mom."

"But you have to go. We all ALWAYS go home for Thanksgiving."

"Why, Mom? There's nothing there for me. All my cousins are younger, and you adults spend most of your time talking about the 'good old days.' I don't even know most of the people you are talking about. And I sit around totally bored, watching a football game I don't even care about. It might be fine for you, but it is the pits for me."

"But you love your grandma, don't you?"

"Yeah, Grandma and Uncle Charlie and all of them—I just don't get my kicks from hanging around them for days with no one there my age."

Mom was getting pretty upset. "But we all bring our children. We like to show off our children. I'm proud of you, honey, and I want the others to see you."

"But, Mom, don't you see? I'm not a child anymore who **89** can just go and show off for the relatives. I'm practically grown. I have my own friends and things I like to do."

Then Mom really did it. She started to cry. "How can you hate my family?" she said.

I felt like such a jerk. But why couldn't she understand? I didn't hate anybody. But I was growing up. Things change. I couldn't be her little girl showing off for the relatives forever.

How could I make her understand?

HOW ABOUT YOU?

Ever get caught between being a child and an adult? Sometimes parents don't know themselves how they see their children. They want them to grow and be on their own, and they want them to stay small like they used to be.

It's hard to be in between—to feel like an adult inside and to be treated like a little child by those around. It's hard to be old and young at the same time, harder yet to help those who can't make up their mind whether they want you to grow or stay small.

HERE'S WHAT I DID

This was not an easy problem for Mom and me to deal with. I guess we're both a little mixed up about whether I am a grown-up or still a child.

To be honest, life was sure a lot easier when I was 12. Mom made all the decisions for me. She told me when to get up, what to wear, where to go. I didn't have to do much thinking. Things seemed a lot safer and simpler then.

Now so much depends on me. Mom can't help with my friends. She doesn't even understand my homework. And I mostly decide for myself where to go and what to do.

But she can't seem to get used to that. She wants to know where I am every minute and what is happening with every person in my life. She tries to "protect" me by keeping me home as much as possible. And sometimes it seems like she is jealous of the time I spend with my friends.

Then, all of a sudden, she is completely turned around. She wants me to be "grown up." She wants me to "take more responsibility."

90

"How can you be grown when your room is such a mess?" she goes. And as we tear the house apart for my constantly disappearing purse, she says rather casually, "Most adults keep track of important things like purses."

The evening after our "discussion" about Thanksgiving, Mom announces, "I'm sorry. You are not going to New York with Robin. You are going home with your father and me. We are a family, and we do things together, and you are going to go with us. And that is final."

I didn't even answer. I just went to my room.

I planned about six different ways to get to New York before my mother would even know about it. I thought that if I got there and called and told her I was there, she might finally realize that I wasn't 12 years old anymore—that I could do things and make decisions on my own. But by the time I got there and called, she'd probably have the National Guard out looking for me in seven states.

The next day, on the way home from school, I stopped at this little jewelry store near home. Sometimes the kids in school buy each other friendship rings. Mostly boys buy them for girls, but anyway, I got one with a little stone in it—not very expensive, but it took the last of my baby-sitting money.

Mom was in the kitchen when I got home. Without a word I handed her the ring box. It wasn't wrapped, so she just opened it and looked inside.

"What's this?" she goes.

"It's a friendship ring," I said, "the kind friends sometimes give to each other."

"Did you spend good money on a ring for somebody at school? Don't you have better things to do with your money? You know you need new clothes. This must have cost $20. Who in the world is a good enough friend to be worth that kind of money?"

"You," I said.

Mom looked at the ring and carefully took it out of the box. She was a lot quieter now. "Me?" she said. "Why me?"

"Mom, when I was 12 I really needed you for a mother, **91** and I probably still do sometimes, but right now, when I'm trying to figure out if I can really be grown and on my own, I need you more for a friend—a good, loving friend."

I don't want you to think that one ring solved the whole problem. I still get mixed up about whether I want to be safe like a child or on my own like an adult. And Mom hasn't got it straight all the time either. She still tries to take care of me and sometimes wants to make my decisions for me. But she is trying.

She called Robin's folks and found out what I would need to take along to New York. And she was wearing the ring when she drove me over to Robin's the day we left.

"I'll tell Grandma you'll try to make it next year," she said.

"Yes, and give them all my love."

"And don't go walking around the city streets at night. It's just not safe, you know. You stay with Robin's parents and stay in at night."

"I will, Mom."

"And remember to wear your raincoat when it . . ."

She was quiet for a minute. "I guess you know about raincoats," she said.

"Yes, Mom. I know."

"Call us at Grandma's when you get to New York."

"I will, Mom."

"I like to know where my friends are and what they are doing," she said.

"I do too, Friend," I said and kissed her good-bye.

She waved a little as she drove away.

"Was your mother crying?" asked Robin.

"I don't know. Maybe. I think she is a little worried about one of her best friends," I said.

"I hope she's all right."

"I hope so too," I said.

SOMETHING TO DO

Mom and I love each other. But sometimes our love seems too small to let each other be what we are. When the love in our family seems too small, I like to read Paul's prayer for "families" in Ephesians 3:14-19. He seems to be praying for us

92

there—praying that we can know how great Christ's love for us is. Then in chapter 4 he tells us what that great growing love in Christ can do in our family. The Spirit helps us be more humble, gentle, and patient with each other, full of His peace that binds us together. You might want to read all of chapters 3 and 4. Perhaps the words will help you too, especially when the love in your family doesn't seem big enough.

Talk to your folks about the way your relationship to each other changes over the years. In what way is a parent's love for a grown child more like love for a friend? How does the love of friends build each other up?

Give your mom or dad a friendship gift.